Copyright © 2019 Paideia Institute for Humanistic Study, Inc.

Text and translation copyright © Michael Fontaine, 2019

Illustration copyright © David Beck, 2019

All rights reserved.

First printing, 2019, New York City

ISBN: 978-1-7324750-7-6

The Paideia Institute for Humanistic Study, Inc.
www.paideiainstitute.org

Pallas, patronus primis punctis proditur.

He used to lead a group devoted to unusual Latin fun,
and he teaches those he fosters about his repeating pig-epic.

In 1530, amid the ferment of the Reformation, the strangest poem in all of Latin literature appeared in bookshops in Antwerp and Augsburg. Titled *Pugna Porcorum—The Pig War*—it consists of 248 dactylic hexameters, every single word of them beginning with the letter *p*. Incredible as it sounds, the poem is a satirical epic telling of a conflict between the corrupt hogs (*porci*), who are hogging all the privileges, and the disgruntled piglets (*porcelli*), who want in on them. It devolves into open war.

The poem was apparently meant as a satire of university life for local enjoyment, but its story has a timeless quality, and—the human condition being what it is—infinite application. And because the principals are all pigs of various kinds, it seems obvious—though it cannot be proven—that it influenced George Orwell in *Animal Farm*.

In this book, I offer the first critical Latin text and translation of the *Pugna* into any language. The author was a minor Belgian (Flemish) friar named John (Johannes) Leo Placentius. Because he wrote under a pseudonym, however, and because his book was instantly pirated and reprinted all over Europe, his true identity was soon lost. First, though, the confusion triggered all kinds of misidentifications, accusations, and recriminations, and, in modern scholarship, at least one hilarious crackpot theory. In the afterword, I explain how it all happened.

The Latin of the *Pugna Porcorum* is insanely hard and every extant copy of the text is corrupt. In rooting through as many as I could, I discovered Placentius revised and reissued his book in 1533 (see the stemma at back). The text that follows is based on that rare second edition.

I would like to thank Dan Gallagher and John Byron Kuhner for help with the Latin. As little pigs, we three first read the *Pugna* at "the Greg" (Rome's Gregorian University) with the patron whose name is encrypted in the dedication; both will spot that and a few other puns in it. I would also like to thank Tyler Patterson, who vetted the manuscript and cleaned up the litter, and especially David Beck, for casting his pearls before us swine.

porcinâ penes Pekingenses periodo MMXIX
prelo Παιδείας prolatum

PUGNA PORCORUM
per
P. Porcium poetam[1]

[Praeterea, **Protestatio** propter puncta perverse posita.
Postremo, **Pasquillus** post prandium Pontificis praelegens poema.][2]

PARACLESIS PRO POTORE

Perlege porcorum pulcherrima proelia, potor.
Potando, poteris placidam proferre poesim.

Potentissimo patrono Porcianorum,
P. Porcius poeta prosperitatem precatur plurimam.

Postquam publice porci putamur, praestantissime patrone, placuit porcorum pugnam poemate pingere, potissime proponendo pericula pinguium praelatorum. Pugnant, pigriter pusillanimes praelati, propter pinguedinis pondus; porro potentius porcelli, pauca proceritate perpoliti. Propterea placeat, precor, puerile poema perlegere, Porcorum Porcellorumque pugnam, propositionibus pictam paribus. Peri perpraepostere.

[PROTESTATIO PLACENTII PROPTER PUNCTA PERVERSE POSITA

Pro patrocinio porcorum plurima prompsi,
    plures producens perbreviansque pedes.
Protervire profunde probas phamamque, proconsul;
    punctula pro placito praecipue posui.
Praefectum posui, praesago pectore pondus;   5
    ponere praeterii per prohibente pedes.][3]

---

1   i.e. *Publium*. The second edition prints *per Placentium Portium poetam* here but retains *Publius* everywhere else.
2   Added in the second edition.
3   Added in the second edition.

THE PIG WAR
by
Publius Porcius the poet

[In addition, a protest on misplaced punctuation.
[In the appendix, Pasquino's reading of a poem after lunch with the Pontifex.]

A SUMMONS TO THE DRINKER

Peruse the pigs' glorious battles, my drinker!
Drinking lets you produce placid poetry.

*For the most mighty patron of the Porciani,
the poet Publius Porcius prays for great prosperity.*[1]

Since we're publicly regarded as pigs, my most illustrious patron, I thought it would be nice to write a poem portraying a *War of the Pigs*, putting special emphasis on the perils faced by the fat bigwigs. The bulkiness of their fat makes sluggish fighters of the cowardly bigwigs, whereas the piglets—thanks to the slight advantage in height they enjoy—fight more nimbly. Accordingly, I hope you'll like reading this silly poem—*The War between the Hogs and Piglets*—which I've narrated in equal episodes. Perish in reverse![2]

[PLACENTIUS' PROTEST ON MISPLACED PUNCTUATION

I came up with a huge number of ideas in enriching my *Pigs*,
    producing too many feet [per line] and cutting them out.
You're fine with my notorious exuberance, my indulgent proconsul,
    but I *was* fastidious in placing my punctuation where I wanted it:
I'd appointed an editor—an expert with good intuition—and,   5
    when he told me not to, I refrained from putting it into the lines.][3]

---

1   A parody of *salutem dat*, "sends greetings/wishes good health." *Porciani* refers to the students of Het Varken college (see the afterword).
2   A parody of *vale*, "farewell!" — The word translated "bigwigs," *praelati* (literally, "the preferred"), can also mean "prelates."
3   Added in the second edition, and not very clear. Placentius is addressing his Antwerp printer, Simon Cock. Apparently struck out extra words by hand in the manuscript he sent him (an overlooked example survives in v. 188, where meter requires the deletion of *poenis*). This interpretation is confirmed by the fact that editions of the "Antwerp 2 litter" do have better punctuation (I have followed or reflected it in the current text).

PRODITUR PATRONUS PORCIANORUM PRIMORDIALIBUS PUNCTIS

Res Inamoena Caret Affectu, Laeta Decorem
Omnimode Aspirat; Bellula Habe Ergo Rata.

PRODITUR POETA

Plura Latent Animo Celata, Et Non Temeranda
Indiciis Ullis; Scilicet hoc volui.

PROLOGUS

Praecelsis proavis pulchre prognate patrone,
pectore prudenti pietateque praedite prisca,
praeter progeniem, praeter praeclara parentum
proelia pro patria, pro praesulibusque peracta,
pleraque pro populo proprio perfecta potenter, 5
pellucens probitate, potenteque prosperitate,
proposito praesente, petens plerumque peritos,
proptereaque probas philomusos, prosequerisque
Parnasso potos pretio precibusque poetas:
postquam percepi puerile placere poema, 10
praecipue propter praescripta prooemia pugnae
porcorum, placuit parvam praefigere pugnae
pagellam, Porcî prodentem proprietates
plausibiles: pinguem patronum promeruisse
pectore pinguiculo—Pol promeruisse—poetam 15
pingui porcorum pingendo poemate pugnam.

PROPOSITIONES PUGNAE

Porcos pistorum pergunt prosternere pugna
porcelli, pasti plantis per pervia prata.

THE INITIALS UNMASK THE PORCIANI'S PATRON

A gloomy thing lacks love, but a happy one radiates beauty
in every direction: so choose pretty things.[4]

THE POET UNMASKED

Many things lie hidden in my heart, and they mustn't be betrayed
by any hints; this was my choice, obviously.[5]

PROLOGUE

My patron, you are the glorious offspring of lofty ancestors
and you possess the prudence and piety of old,
in addition to your noble lineage and the glorious battles
your fathers fought for their country, for their prince-bishops,
and—quite a few of them fought effectively to a total victory—for their own people; 5
you radiate goodness and powerful prosperity,
you typically ask the advice of experts when a proposal is up for deliberation,
and hence you support humanists, and with payments and prayers
you honor poets that drink from Parnassus!
Once I could tell you liked my silly poem   10
(and not least because of the proems that preface *The Pig
War*[6]), I thought it would be nice to add this little page
in to the front of the *War* pointing out your Porcius' impressive
talents: namely, that the poet has earned (yes, *earned!*) himself
the support of a generous and stout patron,   15
simply by telling of a war between pigs in a trivial poem.

THE THEMES[7] OF *THE WAR*

The piglets aim to crush the bakers' hogs in battle,
after feeding on plants in the open meadows.

---

4   The Latin initials spell out RICALDO AB HER, "for Rikald van Heer" (see the afterword). — The false scansion *carēt* is Placentius' mistake; similar oversights appear in lines 88, 143, and 177.
5   The Latin initials spell out PLACENTIUS H[et] V[arken] (see the afterword).
6   This apparently refers to everything on the preceding page (of the first edition), although this prologue seems to address a different patron (see the afterword).
7   A parody of *argumentum*, "plot summary."

PUGNA PORCORUM
per
P. Porcium Poetam

PROCESSUS PORCORUM PONITUR

"Plaudite porcelli, porcorum pigra propago
progreditur!"
        Plures porci pinguedine pleni
pugnantes pergunt: pecudum pars prodigiosa
perturbat pede petrosas plerumque plateas,
pars portentose populorum prata prophanat,   5
pars pungit populando potens, pars plurima plagis
praetendit punire pares, prosternere parvos.
        Primo porcorum praefecti—pectore plano
pistorum porci—prostant, pinguedine pulchri.
Pugnantes prohibent porcellos; ponere poenas   10
praesumunt pravis;
                porro, plebs pessima pergit
protervire prius, post profligare potentes.

THE PIG WAR
by
Publius Porcius the poet

THE HOGS' PROCESSION GETS DISRUPTED

"Clap and cheer, little piglets! The hardy scions of the *hogs*
are coming!"[8]
        Hogs, fat-filled and lots and lots of them,
come marching in, brawling. A huge part of their parcel
are kicking up a ruckus through the cobblestone streets.
Some are desecrating public pasturelands, and it's ugly.   5
A good many are causing damage, while the vast majority
are feinting at peers and pretending to trample the little ones.
At first the hog authorities—the broad-chested
bakers' hogs—step up, and stand out: they're impressive in their bulk.
They shield the piglets from the brawlers, and they're planning   10
to punish the offenders.
        The crowd, though, jumps in boorishly—
jeering at first, then hitting and kicking the elites.

---

8   A breathless announcement as the parade begins.

PROPOSITIO PROCONSULIS

  Proconsul pastus pomorum pulte perorat
PROELIA PRO PECUDE PRAVA PRODESSE; PROINDE,
PROTERVIRE PARUM PATRES PERSAEPE PROBASSE;   15
PORCORUM POPULO PACEM PRIDEM PLACUISSE
PERPETUAM; PACIS PROMI PRAECONIA PASSIM.
  Pro praecone piae pacis per pondera plura
proponente preces, prudens pro plebe patronus
porcus praegrandis profert placidissima pacta.   20

PLACIDA PACTA PROPONUNTUR

  "Pacisci placeat porcis! Per proelia prorsum
plurima priscorum perierunt pascua patrum.
Praestat porcellis potiori pace potiri.
Praestat praelatis primam praebere palaestram."

PLEBS PORCELLORUM PROELIA PORTENDIT

  Porro, proclivis pugnae plebeia potestas   25
proelia portendit, per privilegia prisca
proponens PUGNA PORCOS POTUISSE PATENTI
PROSTRAVISSE PARES, PER PLEBISCITA PROBARI
PORCUM PUGNACEM PECUDEM: "Praeclara potestas
pendet per porcos pugnaces; pergite passim   30
perdere praefectos! Porci properate pusilli
perdere pinguiculos, praefectos praecipitare.
Pigritia pollent praelati perpetuati!"

A SUGGESTION FROM THE GOVERNOR

As he munches apple peels, the governor is pleading with them:
"WARS WAGED AGAINST AN EVIL BRUTE ARE JUST AND GOOD, AND SO IT WAS THAT
OUR FATHERS ELECTED TO STOP MISBEHAVIOR[9] ON NUMEROUS OCCASIONS. 15
FOR A LONG TIME, WE HOGS HAVE ENJOYED PEACE
WITHOUT INTERRUPTION; THE EVIDENCE OF THAT PEACE IS ALL AROUND US."
By dint of his authority, acting as an ambassador of pious peace
and using diplomatic language, a huge hog—a far-seeing patron
of the masses—comes up with an extremely fair compromise: 20

A FAIR COMPROMISE PROPOSED

"Let's us hogs agree to reach a compromise! It was through fighting that
most of our forefathers' fields were lost to us forever.
For our piglets, it's preferable to find a better peace.
For our bigwigs, it's preferable to offer a first-rate school."[10]

THE PIGLET MOB HINTS AT WAR

Itching to fight, though, the powerful mob 25
is hinting at war. In accordance with their time-honored privileges
they're arguing, WE CAN CRUSH THE HOGS—
OUR *EQUALS!*—IN AN OPEN[11] BATTLE; THEIR DECISIONS
PROVE THE HOG IS A VIOLENT ANIMAL: "Their *glorious* authority
rests on hog *force*! Join in, destroy their commanders 30
at random! Act fast and destroy them,
you puny pigs, trample their fat commanders!
Laziness perpetuates these bigwigs in power!"

---

9   i.e. encroachment, trespass.
10   Or perhaps "a level playing field."
11   The second edition reads "in all-out (*potenti*) war," but this may be a typo rather than a revision (cf. 212), and it's hard to choose between the two.

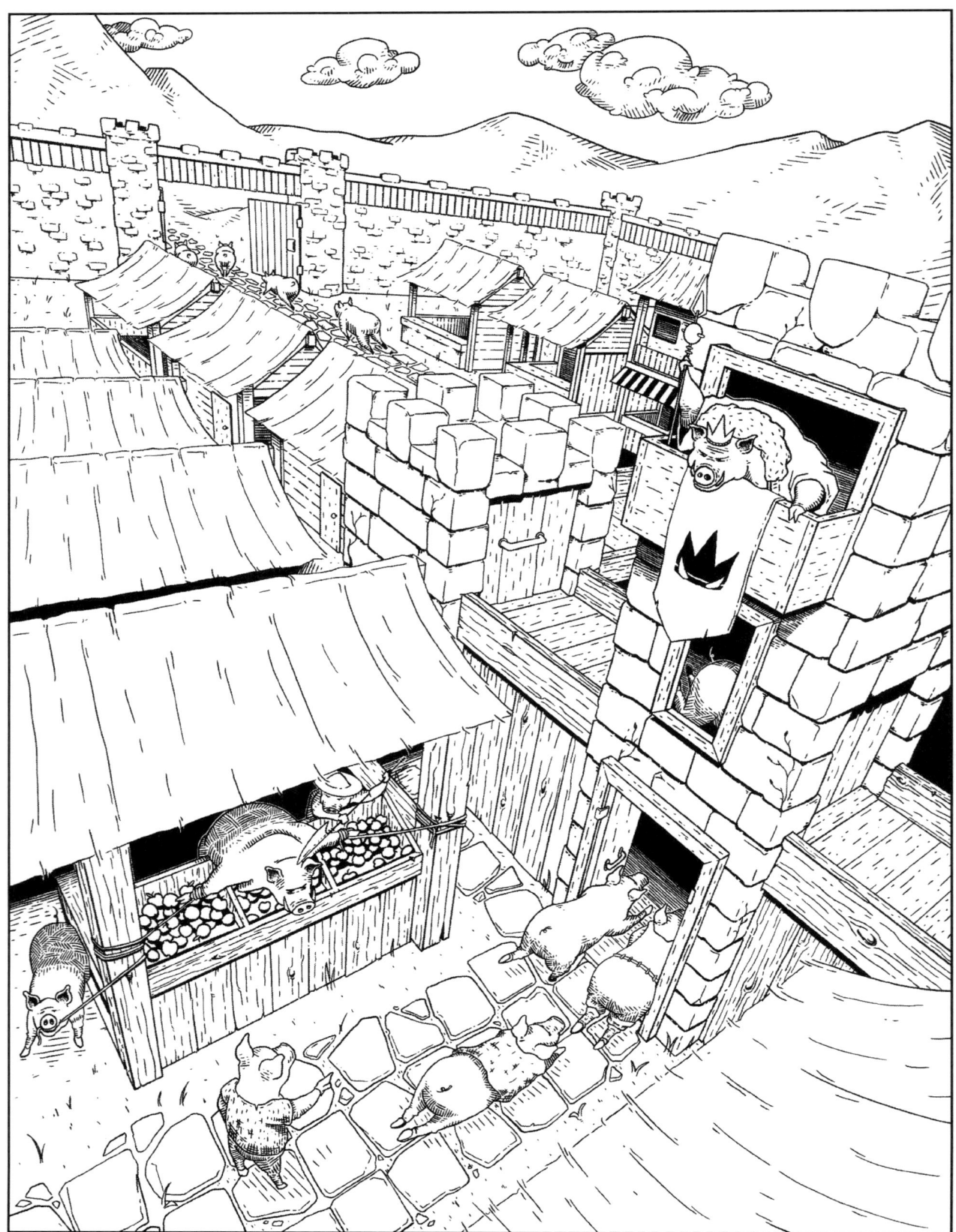

PRAEPROPERA PORCELLORUM PENETRATIO

   Postquam plebs pertaesa potentatus penetravit,
praecipiti pede porcelli petiere pusilli.   35
Pugnando properare prius, pessumdare patres:
praestituunt personatos praecurrere porcos
propugiles. Porro, plenum pinguedine putri
praelatum porcum pistrino pinsere panem
praecipiunt; per posticam, per pervia portant.   40

A SUDDEN ATTACK BY THE PIGLETS

   The mob had grown sick of the regime and once it pushed its way in,
the puny piglets charged, running willy-nilly.   35
They proved faster in the fighting, flattening their fathers.
They order some in disguise to dispatch the hogs' elite guard
by surprise. Then, they order the bakery's bigwig—
a flabby, fat-filled hog—to start baking bread.
They're frog-marching him through the streets and in through the back door.   40

PRECES PROCONSULIS PRO PRAELATIS

Propterea properans, proconsul poplite prono
praecipitem plebem pro patrum pace poposcit.
"Persta paulisper, pubes pretiosa, precamur!
Pensa profectum parvum pugnae peragendae.
Plures plorabunt, postquam praecelsa premetur   45
praelatura patrum; porcelli percutientur
passim, posteaquam pingues porci periere.
Propterea petimus: praesentem ponite pugnam.
Per pia porcorum petimus penetralia! Posthac
praelati poterint[4] patrata piacula parce   50
perpetrare; procul postponite proelia prava;
prae praelatorum poenis patientia praestat."

PROPOSITIONES PORCELLORUM

Plebs porcellorum pariter praecone parato
porcis praelatis proponit particulares

PARTICULAE PACIS

pacis particulas: PATEANT PRAESENTIA PACTA   55
PORCORUM POPULO, PORCORUM POSTERITATI.
"Principio, petimus praelatos perpetuatos
postponi, propter pia privilegia patrum.
Porcellos patuit pariformi pondere pastos
porcis persimiles, porcos praestare pusillos   60
propter pulmonem, propter penetrale palati:
pars parvi porci prunis plerumque perusta
principibus primis portatur. Porro, putrescens
porcorum pectus putri pinguedine plenum
proicitur passim; partim pro peste putatur.   65
Propterea, porcis praelatio praeripiatur.
Pergite, porcelli, praefectos praecipitare!"

---

4 Placentius writes *poterint* (for *poterunt*) consistently; it appears twice more below (in all editions). I have not changed it.

THE GOVERNOR PLEADS ON BEHALF OF THE BIGWIGS

Hurrying on that account, the governor knelt down and
pleaded with the furious mob for peace for their fathers.
"*Stop* for a moment, dear boys! Please, I beg you!
Think of how little progress will come from finishing this war.
Many will protest when their fathers' elite privileges 45
get cut off. Piglets will get slain[12]
all over, once the fat hogs have been finished off.
For that reason, I beg you: call off this impending war—
in the name of the hogs' holy temples, I beg you! Going forward, 50
the bigwigs will get to perpetrate the crimes they've committed
only rarely. Call off this evil war, put it far from your mind!
Patience is preferable to punishing bigwigs."

THE PIGLETS' PROPOSAL

The mob of piglets, having secured a diplomat of their own,
propose to the hog bigwigs specific articles of peace:

THE ARTICLES OF PEACE

THE PRESENT TREATY SHALL BE AVAILABLE 55
TO THE HOGS AS A WHOLE AND TO THE HOGS' POSTERITY:—
"First, we demand an end to bigwigs being
automatically appointed because of their fathers' pious privileges.
We've seen that piglets who get to eat an equal amount are
virtually on par with hogs, and that they're *better* than puny hogs 60
because of their lungs and the inside of their mouths;
in the case of a little hog, part tends to get barbecued on briquettes
and served up to princes of the first rank, while the rotting
breast of a hog, which is full of flabby fat,
just gets thrown out (it's partly thought to spread disease). 65
Accordingly, the privileges must be wrested from the hogs!
Go, my piglets, chuck the bosses out!"

---

12   Revised in the second edition to "Piglets will suffer grievously (*perpetientur*)".

POSTERIOR PUGNA

      Pro praelatura porci pugnare parati
prosiliunt: pars prata petit, pars prona paludes.
Prodit praecipuo proterva potentia plausu.   70
Porro, porcelli pulchre per prata perurgent
pinguiculos properare procul. Penetrare parati
per portas patulas, porcos perfodere pergunt.
Prosternunt: pinguedo potens prohibet properare.

PORCI PACISCI PETUNT

      Propterea, pacem proponunt: "Parcite porcis,   75
porcelli! Posthac, potiemur pace perenni."
Propterea, pulcher porcellus praeco politus
prospiciens patres pronos peccata profari,
prospiciens positos praedae, positosque periclo,
propositum pandit: "Pacem perferre potestis?   80
Parcite, praelati. Procerum pondus puerile
perdurare parum propter plerosque putatur:
perfringunt pacem penitus post pacta peracta.

PRAECONIS PROPOSITIO

Ponite pro pacto pignus: proferte potentes
pro pacis praxi. Potiora pericula pensant   85
porcelli; portent pignus; pax pacta placebit."

THE SECOND BATTLE

   Prepared to fight for their privileges, the hogs
leap forward. Some head for the meadows, some bolt headlong for the marshes.
Their forces advance, ululating with war whoops.   70
In the meadows, though, the piglets are gloriously forcing
the fatties to flee far away. Already prepared to run in
through the open gates, they begin goring the hogs,
they're mowing them down; their mighty corpulence prevents the hogs from fleeing.

THE HOGS SUE FOR PEACE

   Therefore, they call for a ceasefire. "Spare us hogs,   75
piglets! Henceforth, we'll have permanent peace."
Therefore, a handsome piglet, a well-mannered diplomat,
seeing their fathers inclined to admit their mistakes,
seeing them poised for plunder and poised for danger,
reveals a proposal: "Can you actually put up with peace?   80
Give me a break, bigwigs! A silly promise made by leaders,
experience shows, isn't known for lasting very long:
they totally violate the peace the moment the treaty's been ratified!

THE DIPLOMAT'S PROPOSAL

Put up *collateral* for your treaty; hand over your *leaders*
to effect your peace. Piglets prefer proof;   85
let them come up with collateral; a treaty, duly ratified, will satisfy us."

PROFERTUR PIGNUS PRO PACTIONE

   Princeps porcorum propria pro plebe pedestri
procumbens, paenē perplexus, proelia propter
pestiferi populi, promittit praemia pulchra:
pultem pomorum, propinam pulvere pisti   90
pastilli, partem placentae posterioris,
pocula profundae perquam pretiosa paludis.
Porcum praegrandem placido pro pignore praebet,
promulgans PLENA PORCELLOS PROPRIETATE
PRAEFECTURARUM POSTHAC PERTINGERE PALMAM.   95
Porro, porcelli pinxere prooemia pacis
particulis paribus: PATEAT PAX POSTERITATI.

PARTICULAE PACTAE PACIS

   Porci praelati placido pacto pepigerunt
perpetuam pacem, POSTHAC PRAECEDERE PARVOS
PORCELLOS, PORCOS PUTRI PINGUEDINE PLENOS;   100
PHAS POSTHAC, PORCIS PASSIM PUGNARE PUSILLIS
PRO POMIS PUTRIDIS, PRO PORTAE POSTERIORIS
PROVENTU PINGUI; POTERINT PURGARE PLATEAS;
PROLIXE POTERINT POMARIA PARTICIPARE;
PARTIRI PRAEDAS, PATULAS PERAGRARE PALUDES.   105
Proclamaturi porcelli pectore pleno,
postquam praeripitur porcellis per peregrinos,
postquam percipiunt pede prendi posteriori.

COLLATERAL FOR THE DEAL IS COME UP WITH

   Prostrating himself on behalf of his own mass of soldiers,
the hogs' leader, practically at a loss because of the battles
this damned race of people has brought him, promises very fine rewards:
apple peels, the offering of a dust-beaten   90
loaf of bread, part of a day-old cake,
priceless drinks of boundless marsh-water.
He offers a colossal hog as a docile hostage,
proclaiming that WITH FULL PROPRIETARY RIGHTS,
PIGLETS SHALL HENCEFORTH ATTAIN THE HONOR OF HIGH OFFICES.   95
The piglets then embellished the treaty's preamble
with an article of their own: MAY THIS PEACE ENDURE FOR POSTERITY!

THE ARTICLES OF THE PEACE TREATY

The hog bigwigs agreed upon a perpetual peace
in their placid treaty, that:

- HENCEFORTH, LITTLE **PIGLETS** TAKE PRECEDENCE OVER FLABBY, FAT-FILLED **HOGS**.   100
- HENCEFORTH, IT IS RIGHT AND PROPER FOR PUNY **HOGS** TO SQUABBLE
  OVER ROTTEN APPLES, OVER RICH SLOPS THROWN OUT THE BACK DOOR.
  - THEY SHALL GET TO CLEAN THE STREETS;
  - THEY SHALL GET TO COURTEOUSLY SHARE THE ORCHARDS.
  - THEY SHALL SHARE SCRAPS AND PASS ON THROUGH AVAILABLE MARSHES. 105

The piglets were about to hail the terms, their chests puffing,
when the piglets get preempted by their grunts[13],
as they realize they're being grabbed by their hind feet.

---

13 These *peregrini* seem to be not "foreigners" but "raw" recruits, i.e. grunts, rank-and-file soldiers, who want to celebrate; they return in vv. 167-210; they are not the razorbacks of v. 157.

POMPAE PORCELLORUM POST PACTAM PACEM PERACTAE

    "Plaudite porcelli, plebes pretiosa! Perenni
parta pace, parate procul praeludia pulchra: 110
pompas praecipuas, proscaenia publica palmae,
purpureos pannos! Picturas pendite pulchras
progeniem priscam porcellorum perhibentes.
Priventur platani, priventur pondere pinus.
Porcellis passim pomaria prostituantur.   115
Palmarum prorsus plantatio praeripiatur
pendula; pro pacta portentur pace parati
palmarum pilei. Procedat pulchra propago
pacificatorum porcellorum penetrando
planitiem patriae passim, peragrando plateas.   120
Plantae pro pedibus plateatim proiciantur!
    "Portetur per praecipuos praeco peramoenus,
pacis perfector. Promat praeconia pacis
publicitus; prono procumbant poplite porci;
porcellos patriae patronos profiteantur!   125

THE PIGLETS' VICTORY PARADE, MARKING THE CONCLUSION OF THE PEACE TREATY

    "Clap and cheer, piglets, my precious people! Now that you've obtained
permanent peace, prepare a fine celebration in the distance: 110
A glorious parade! Competitive shows for the people!
Crimson clothes! Put beautiful paintings on display
to trumpet the piglets' venerable lineage!
Let plane trees and pine trees be stripped of their weight![14]
Let the orchards be opened up for any and all piglets to enjoy!   115
Let plantings of palm trees be totally plundered
of their branches! To mark your ratified treaty, let garlands of freedom and triumph
be made from palms, and worn. The glorious race of piglets,
having made peace, should parade everywhere they like, entering
their country's meadows, strolling through its streets.   120
Let plants be thrown before your feet from street to street!
    "Let dignitaries sweep your magnificent diplomat aloft,
the engineer of our peace treaty! Let him issue proclamations of the peace
publicly; let the hogs prostrate themselves on bended knee,
let them acknowledge that the *piglets* are the masters of this country!   125

---

14   i.e., branches and foliage.

PINCERNA PRAECEDIT PRAECONEM
POCULO PLENISSIMO

"Porro, praecedat potu pincerna paludis
pocula propinans plenissima, pabula praebens
pulmenti putris pro proprietate palati.
Pro praecone, potens paleae pistura paretur,
proluvies pepli polluti, portio pinguis 130
pleni potoris promentis particulatim
pocula praesumpta, praegustatos patinarum
pullos, perdices, pavos, porcos piperatos.
"Praeterea, patriae per prima palatia pergat
persuadens populo porcellorum pietatem. 135
Plaudant porcelli, portent per plaustra patronum;
per patriam patulo processu perspiciatur.
Pistorum porci prope pistrinum patiantur
perpetuas poenas, praeservati prope postes.
Perturbent pueri porcos pede percutiendo. 140
Propellant porcos pulchrae per pensa puellae;

PORCELLI PUELLARUM POLLICE PERFRICTI PROCUMBUNT

pertractent parvos porcellos pollice prono.
Procumbent; pīlos patientur pectine pecti."
    Plaudite, porcelli! Pistorum plangite porci!
Pistores pascant porcos pastu palearum, 145
percussos partim pedibus, per plurima probra,
partim proiectos petris pugnisque pedoque.
Pastores pascant porcellos prosperitate
praecipua, peragrantes prata patentia passim.

THE CUPBEARER MARCHES AHEAD OF THE DIPLOMAT, HIS GOBLET BRIMMING

  "Furthermore, ahead of him should march a cupbearer, pouring
goblets brimming with water to drink, offering food—
rotten slops, which are just right for our palate.
For our diplomat, get a mighty serving of milled straw,
the discharge of a dirty garment, a healthy helping   130
of a nauseous drinker's barfing up, bit by bit,
the drinks he's downed, and the frying pans' leftover
chickens, partridges, peacocks, and peppered pork.
  "Next, he should head to our country's main courts
and persuade the people of the piglets' piety.   135
Piglets should clap, cheer, and parade their patron around in a wagon.
Throughout the country, let him be gazed upon in a pompous procession!
Near the bakery, the bakers' hogs should suffer
perpetual punishment, on display near the doorway.
Boys should harass the hogs by kicking them!   140
Pretty girls should chase the hogs through their spinning,

THE PIGLETS GET MASSAGES FROM THE THUMBS OF GIRLS, AND RELAX

but they can massage little piglets with the tips of their thumbs.
They'll lie down, relaxing, and let their combs card their hair out."
  Clap and cheer, piglets! Lament, o bakers' hogs!
The bakers can go feed the hogs a meal of chaff,   145
now that some have gotten kicked for their many, many misdeeds,
and some have gotten chased away with stones and fists and sticks.
Let shepherds feed the piglets with their special
abundance, as they go wandering through open meadows as they will.

PORCORUM PRAESAGA PENSICULATIO PRO PRAEFECTURA PARANDA

    Postridie, postquam porcelli pace potiti,   150
praesumpsere patres proterve pungere passim,
proelia praedictae pugnae populis perhibentes.
Plurima porcorum pensans, praesaga potestas
proposuit primo, PALMAE PRAESCRIBERE PONDUS
PESTIFERAE PLEBI PORCELLORUM PEDETEMPTIM;   155
proposuit PEDITES PRETIO PRO POSSE PARARE,
PORCOS PRAEDONES PER PAGOS PERQUE PALUDES
PUNGENTES PECUDES PROMUSCIDE; phamaque passim

THE HOGS PLOT TO GET THEIR PRIVILEGES BACK

    The next day—a day after the piglets had gotten their peace treaty—   150
their fathers had the chutzpah to spread trouble everywhere,
telling the world about the fighting in the aforementioned war.
Weighing lots and lots of considerations, the hogs' far-seeing authorities
schemed, first to GRADUALLY DISPUTE THE IMPORTANCE
OF THE VICTORY WITH THAT DAMNED DIRTY RABBLE OF PIGLETS;   155
it resolved to HIRE AS MERCENARIES, AT A PRICE WE CAN AFFORD,
THE RAZORBACK BANDITS THAT HARASS TAME ANIMALS WITH THEIR SNOUTS
IN THE COUNTRYSIDE AND MARSHES; — and the rumor's running

PHAMA PROELII

perfertur, properatque pecus proclive. Proinde,
praeficitur pennae procurator peracutus,   160
ponens pugnaces porcos pecudesque papyro.
Promittunt posito pede praefectis PROPERARE
PRAESCRIPTO PUGILUM, PUGNAM PRAESTARE PARATI
PRAECIPUAM PROUT PRAECIPIENT PRINCEPS PUGILESQUE.

PERFIDIA PRAEFECTORUM PRETIUM PRAERIPIENTIUM PUGNANTIBUS

    Porro, proventus pretii plerisque parantur.   165
Praecurrunt proceres, pretii plus percipientes.
Placant pollicitis (proh!) paupellos peregrinos:
perfidiam patrant, proprioque penu potiores
praestituunt praedas. Proponunt postea plebi
persolvendarum propinarum paraclesim,   170
pugnaque protrahitur.

PORCUS PHILOMUSUS PROMOTUS PARISIIS

    Porro, porcus philomusus
—paedotriba pusillorum, per Parisienses
promotus, pagi pastor, parochusque paludis,
Paulum perdoctus pariter producere Petrum—
protestabatur. "Proh! perdita pectora plena   175
perfidiae: pudeat perceptae praemia praedae
plebi praeripere peccato pernicioso.
Peccatis! Prodet profusa pecunia, prodet,
prodet praedones, postquam poscent peregrini
praemia pro pugna patrata, proque periclis."   180

"WAR!"

rampant! And the herd is stampeding for it! Accordingly,
a very smart overseer is put in charge of the pen;[15] 160
he's arranging the combat hogs and regulars on paper.
Planting a foot, they swear an oath to the colonels to SNAP INTO ACTION
UPON OUR PLATOON'S COMMAND, PREPARED AS WE ARE TO PUT UP A GLORIOUS
FIGHT PRECISELY AS OUR OFFICER AND PLATOON SHALL ORDER US TO.

THE TWO-TIMING COLONELS STEAL THEIR SOLDIERS' PRIZES

Next, stocks of prizes are procured for a great many pigs, but 165
the leaders run up to the front and take most of the prizes.
They placate the powerless grunts with—alas!—promises:
two-timing them, they promise plunder better than
their own provisions. They offer the commoners
an I.O.U. to pay their pledges later, 170
and the fight goes on.

THE PARIS-PROMOTED HUMANIST HOG

A humanist hog, however,
—a teacher of children, promoted by the
Parisians, a country priest, a marshland pastor,
trained (and well) to recite Paul and Peter equally—
was protesting[16]: "Alas! Criminals! Hearts full 175
of treachery! You should be ashamed of wresting the rewards
of the plunder you filched by this pernicious sin.
You are committing a sin! Spending the money will unmask—*unmask!*—
UNMASK! you bandits when the grunts demand
payment for fighting this battle and facing these perils." 180

---

15 i.e., drawing up a plan of attack.
16 If the humanist hog alludes to any real figure, it can only be Juan Luis Vives (1493-1540), some of whose life circumstances match the description (see Marín Ibáñez 1994).

PROPALATIO PERFIDIAE PER PHILOMUSUM

    Personuit parochus, pergens proponere plures
perfidiae partes; porro, princeps pugilesque
PESTIFERUM PAROCHUM proclamabant PERIMENDUM,
PSEUDOEVANGELICUMque probabant PRAECIPITANDUM
PONTO; praeterea, PLUS PROVENISSE PERICLI   185
PERSUASU PAROCHI, PLUS PONDERIBUS PAVIMENTI
PORTAE PRAECELSAE, PLUS PULVERIBUS PLATEARUM.
Protestabantur [poenis][5] PLECTENDUM, POSTE PATENTE;
PONENDUM PROPE PRUNAS, PARTICULISQUE PERUSTIS
PROFUNDO PUTEO PROFUNDE PRAECIPITANDUM.   190

THE HUMANIST EXPOSES THE TWO-TIMING

    Thus the pastor shouted, proceeding to lay out more
details of their two-timing. But the commander and platoon
kept proclaiming THIS TROUBLESOME PASTOR NEEDS TO DIE!
and liked the idea of HURLING HIS FALSE GOSPEL
INTO THE SEA! Furthermore, TOO MUCH DANGER HAS COME   185
FROM THIS PASTOR'S PERSUASIONS—MORE THAN THE WEIGHT OF THE STONEWORK
OF A TOWERING ARCHWAY, MORE THAN THE DUST IN THE STREETS.
They kept protesting that HE MUST BE PUNISHED ON A PUBLIC WHIPPING POST;
HE SHOULD BE PLACED ON BURNING COALS, AND WHEN HIS BITS HAVE BURNED UP
HE SHOULD BE THROWN HEADFIRST DEEP DOWN A DEEP WELL.   190

---

5   See n. 3 of the translation; the unmetrical *poenis* appears in every printing.

POENA PHILOMUSI

Publicitus pugiles praedicta piacula patrant,
plebsque putat pulchrum, philomusum perdere porcum.
      Proinde, preces princeps proponit, plebsque parata
promittit parere piis precibus, pugilesque
partiri pergunt propinam, perficiuntque   195

PORCELLORUM PRACTICA PERCIPIENTIUM PERSOLUTIONIS PERFIDIAM

      perfidiam; pauci prohibent peccata patrari:
pro placito pugilum, plecti plerique putantur
PROPTER PERFIDIAM PROPALATAM PEREGRINIS.

PONITUR PERSOLUTIO PERQUAM PRAESENTISSIMA

      Postquam porcelli perceperunt peregrinos
privari pretio, prolixe pensiculando   200
publicitus propere procurant praemia pugnae
proponi porcis paganis. Persoluturus,
prostat praeco potens; plures praecurrere porci
praetendunt, prohibetque pedo plus percipientes.
      Postquam pellecti pretio porci peregrini   205
praesidium pugnae praebebant: praecipitare
pugnam pergebant porci.

PINGUES PORCI PROVEHUNTUR PLAUSTRIS

      Porro, properabant
partim pinguiculi, partim putredine pleni
provecti plaustris; partim pedites properabant.
Porro, porcelli praeceperunt peregrinis   210
plaustra penetrando porcos prosternere pingues
producique palam pendendos poste patente.

THE HUMANIST PUNISHED

The platoon exacts the aforementioned punishments in public,
and the rabble thinks it's a glorious thing, destroying the humanist hog.
     Accordingly, the commander proposes prayers, and the rabble readily
swears oaths of loyalty to obey, and the platoon
proceeds to celebrate a toast, and they make their two-timing complete.   195

THE PIGLETS' ACTION IN SPOTTING
THE TWO-TIMING ON THE PAYMENT[17]

     Few stop horrible mistakes from being perpetrated:
it's thought a great many wind up punished, on the platoon's orders,
FOR EXPOSING OUR TWO-TIMING TO THE GRUNTS.

A FIX IS PROPOSED RIGHT THEN AND THERE

     Once the piglets saw the grunts
were getting cheated of their pay, they brainstorm ideas and   200
hastily arrange for combat pay at state expense to be
offered to the country hogs. To pay it out,
a powerful spokesman steps up; lots and lots of hogs vie
to run up first, and he stops them with a stick from taking more.
     Once the hogs' grunts were won over by the pay,   205
they started offering protection in a fight: the hogs
were trying to spark another war!

THE FAT HOGS RIDE OUT IN WAGONS

     What's more, coming at them were
the plumpers on one side, on another the flab-filled fatsos
riding in wagons, and from another, soldiers were coming on foot.
The piglets, though, instructed their grunts   210
to board the wagons, knock the fat hogs down,
and drag them out to hang on a public whipping post.

---

17   This subheading refers to vv. 199ff, but I have not ventured to move it.

PRAEDATIO PORCELLORUM

  Propterea, pedites prudenter progredientes
perturbaverunt proieceruntque potenter
plaustrum porcorum, praedaque potente potiti,   215
praecipuos porcos pertraxerunt plateatim.
Porro, porcorum prospecto principe primo,
praeco potens populo propinavit PERIMENDUM,
PLECTENDUM POENIS, PENDENDUM POSTE PATENTE.
  Porro, pauca petit princeps proferre priusquam   220
perficiat placitum praeconis plebs pileata,
permittuntque parum proponere; proinde profatur:

PRECATIO PRINCIPIS PORCORUM

  "Parcite, porcelli! Proavorum prisca putamur
progenies; prisci potuerunt plura parentes
proelia pro patria patrare, pericula plura   225
pro populo perferre pio, pro plebe parati
poenas pauperiemque pati. Possunt pietatem
publica phana parentum pyramidesque probare.
Promeriti pulchre, per praemia picta probantur.
Propterea, pensate, precor, pensate periclum!   230
Parcite perdendo, pietatem perficientes."
  Postquam perfecit princeps praedicta, parumper
plorans, percutiensque palam pectus peramoenum,
profert PARCENDUM PLORANTI praeco politus
PROPTER PROGENIEM, PROPTER PRETIOSA POTENTUM   235
PATRUM PRIVILEGIA, PROGNATUMque profatur
PROGENIE PROPRIA. Princeps praecoque proinde

PACISCUNTUR PRINCIPES

pergunt pacisci, populo prope prospiciente:
PRAELATOS PARITER, PRAELATIS PARTICIPARI,
PARTIRI PRAEDAS. Porro, promiscua pubes   240
propterea profert, "Pereat praelatio prava!"

THE PIGLETS PLUNDER

      Therefore, the foot soldiers, advancing cautiously,
shook and in a show of strength flipped
the hogs' wagon on its side; and, after collecting rich spoils,   215
they frog-marched the hog heroes through the streets.
When he spotted the hogs' main commander, however,
the mighty spokesman swore to the people that HE DESERVES EXECUTION,
DESERVES BEATINGS AND PUNISHMENT, DESERVES TO HANG ON A PUBLIC WHIPPING POST.
      The commander, though, asks to offer them a few things before   220
the mob, wearing their bonnets of freedom, carries out the spokesman's will,
and they allow him to make a short proposal. Accordingly, he says:

THE PLEA OF THE HOG COMMANDER

      "Stop, piglets, spare me! I am held to be our ancestors'
original offspring; my forefathers were able
to wage lots and lots of battles for our country, to endure lots and lots   225
of dangers for their loyal nation. For their people, they were ready
to suffer punishment and poverty. Our parents' public shrines
and pyramids can prove their devotion.
Their glorious services to the state are proven by prize paintings.
Please, therefore, think—think of the danger!   230
Do not destroy me in order to demonstrate your piety."[18]
      After the commander finished the aforementioned words, wailing
a bit and openly beating his beautiful breast,
the polished spokesman proposes SPARING THIS FELLOW WEEPING
BECAUSE OF HIS LINEAGE, BECAUSE OF HIS MIGHTY FATHERS'   235
PRECIOUS PRIVILEGES, and he proclaims him
AN OFFSPRING OF MY OWN LINE.
      Accordingly, the commander and the spokesman

THE LEADERS COME TO AN AGREEMENT

proceed to make an agreement as the people look closely on:
"BIGWIGS SHALL DIVIDE AND SHARE IN PLUNDER WITH BIGWIGS
ON EQUAL TERMS." For that reason, though, the young folks,   240
joining together, cry out, "*Damn* these corrupt privileges!"

---

18   Revised in the second edition to "Spare this commander (*praefecto*)! Perfect your piety!"

POPULI PROPOSITIO POTISSIMA

  Postquam parturiunt praeclara penaria praedas,
perficiunt pacem pariter, patitur populusque.
Posteaquam patuit praerepta pecunia plebi,
pangunt privatam procerum praecordia pacem: 245
plectunt periuros periuria plura patrantes.
Propterea, porci, porcelli, plebs, populusque
posthac principibus prohibent producere pugnam.

PERSONUIT PLACENTIUS POST POCULA

Potentissimo, pientissimo, prudentissimoque principi, patri purpurato, praesenti
Pontifici, Placentius plurimum precatur prosperitatis.

  Perge, pater patriae, patriarum perfice pacem.
Promereare palam palmam, placidissime princeps,
possessae pacis. Primam perhibe pietatem
priscorum patrum per prudentissima pacta.
  Posteritas perget praeconia promere passim   5
pontifici pretiosa pio. Plebecula, pubes,
primores patriae proclamabunt peramoeno
plausu pastorem pacis, pia pectora plaudent.
  Phama peragrabit, peragrabit phama polorum
per penetralia. Praeterea, populosa propago,   10
progenies patriae, patres, puerique pusilli
protestabuntur priscis patribus potiorem
pontificem pileo pretioso praedominantem.
  Phama penetrabit, penetrabit phama paludes
Persarum. Poterit phoenix proferre perennis   15
pacis particulas, per pontificale paratas
praesidium. Posthac, penetrabit pax paradisum.
  Plebs peregrinorum prospecta pace perenni
placati populi pactum pariforme probabit.
Publica patronum pacis, privata parentem   20
pectora, perpetuo plausu, pariter perhibebunt.
  Prudens pontificis pectus per plura probetur
plectra poetarum; plerique poemata promant.

A POWERFUL PROPOSAL FROM THE PEOPLE

Once the excellent pantries have been delivered of their spoils,
they make a peace treaty on equal terms, and the people agree to it.
After the money that had been stolen from the commoners appears,
the leaders' minds agree to a private treaty: 245
they punish the traitors who'd done lots and lots of double-timing.
Therefore the hogs, the piglets, the commoners, and the nation
henceforth prohibit their leaders from producing a fight.

A POSTSCRIPT FROM PLACENTIUS, ADDED AFTER DRINKING

To the mightiest, most pious, and wisest prince, purple-robed father[19], and present pontifex[20], Placentius prays for supreme prosperity.

Carry on, father of our country, and perfect the peace of nations!
May you openly earn the palm prize, most placid prince,
of the peace you possess. Advertise your forefathers'
first-rate piety in most provident treaties.
Posterity will go on to produce constant proclamations 5
that are precious to a pious pontifex. The people, young folks, and
aristocrats of our country will hail their
shepherd of peace with delightful applause; pious hearts will clap and cheer.
Your phame will spread out, out will your phame spread through the homes
of the heavens. Furthermore, your many offspring, 10
our country's future—fathers and little children—
will declare you a better pontifex than their forefathers,
one who rules by his precious bonnet of freedom.
Your phame will push on into, on will your phame push into the
Persian Gulf. The phoenix will be able to proffer 15
the details of your enduring peace treaty, the product of pontifical
protection. After that, your peace will push on into heaven.
The great mass of foreigners will approve an identical pact,
having foreseen the enduring peace of a nation you subdued.
With unceasing applause and in equal measure, public hearts 20
will call you the patron of peace; private hearts will call you their father.
Let our pontifex's prudent heart be celebrated by poets'
many lyres! Let lots of them produce poems!

---

19 i.e. both leader and priest.
20 i.e. prince-bishop, not pope.

(a priore pagina progreditur)

Praecipuam plerique parentelae probitatem
pertractent prosa, praestante poemate prorsus. 25
Praecellat princeps pacis, princeps pietatis.

POSTREMO PRONUNTIAVIT

Pensa pauperiem, princeps praeclare, poetae!

PRECATIUNCULA
P. PORCII POETAE

Parce, precor, pingui pagellae; parce pudendae
    pugnantium paroemiae.
Parce parum pulchrae picturataeque poesi,
    praesente pictae poculo.
Phoebo postposito placuit profundere plura 5
    praeceps, poemaque promere.
Postquam potaram, perlegi paucula puncta
    pingens, proindeque potitans.
Perplacuit poto plusquam puerile poema,
    plerisque persuadentibus, 10
produxique palam perscrutandum paradigma,
    pleno probandum poculo.
Percusso pluteo puduit puduitque papyri,
    partique pudet poematis.
Porro, potores partim prodire perurgent, 15
    partim precantur protinus,
praesertimque potest patronus praecipiendo
    parva precatus pagina.
Porcorum populus, porcellorumque precatur
    promiscue plebecula, 20
perfectam pugnam perfecto ponere prelo
    propediem Placentium.

(proceeding from the previous page)

Let lots of them treat of your parent's special probity
in prose and in absolutely outstanding poetry.   25
May the prince of peace and prince of piety prevail!

HIS CLOSING PRONOUNCEMENT

My illustrious prince, don't forget your poet's poverty!

A HUMBLE REQUEST FROM PUBLIUS PORCIUS THE POET

Please be nice to my silly pamphlet; be nice to my embarrassing[21]
    parable of people fighting.
Be nice to its unpretty and clumsily adorned poetry,
    which I worked on with a glass of wine in hand.
Putting Phoebus second[22], I chose to pour out many bits   5
    fast and furiously, and to come out with a poem.
After I'd finished drinking, I read a few points carefully,
    working on them, and then drinking some more.
In my drunkenness, I *really* liked my silly poem a lot,
    and with quite a few people talking me into it,   10
I produced a sample for public scrutiny,
    which needed a full glass of wine to like.
I was ashamed of losing my inhibitions and ashamed of my paper,
    and I'm ashamed this poem was born.
However, drinkers are partly pushing for it to be published,   15
    and partly begging me nonstop,
and by giving the order, a patron really can [make it happen],
    when a humble page asks him to.
The nation of hogs[23] and the great mass of piglets are united in asking
    that Placentius send his finished *Battle* to the perfect   20
    printing press any day now.

---

21   Translating the transmitted *pudendae*. It is tempting to interpret it as the adverb *pudende*, "people fighting shamefully," but there are no other instances of *e* spelled *ae* in *The Pig War*.
22   i.e., worrying less about the poetry. As the god of (polished) poetry, Phoebus Apollo is typically set in opposition to Dionysus/Bacchus, god of wine and ecstasy.
23   i.e. the residents of Het Varken, the *Porciani*.

[PASQUILLUS PRONUNTIABAT POST PRANDIUM PONTIFICIS PRAEFIXAM PAGELLAM

Praelatimastix praeco placitusque poeta,
    Principibus pridem Pontificique placens,
Peligni patitur poenas probrumque poetae:
    proscriptus, patitur praemia promeritus.
Propterea patribus patres parere pusillos 5
    persuadet propera prosperitate proba.]⁶

FINIS

Carus centurio curavit comere chartas
censorem, curae commisit chalcographorum.

AD LECTOREM, IACOBUS DESCHAMPS⁷

Porciolus porcos, cecinisti parva croacum.
    Sic condigna refert praemia, Homere, tibi.

AD EUNDEM

Maeonides ranas cecinit sed Porcius illo
    posterior porcos. Plaudite utrique, precor.

AD EUNDEM

Potando pugnas porcorum perlege, potor: 5
    potanti posuit praemia Porciolus,
porcorumque procul propellunt proelia planctus:
    persuadent propter poemata praecinere.
Perdocuit paucis porcorum pulchra poeta
    proelia; perlecto plaudite Porciolo. 10

---

6   Added in the second edition.
7   In the Paris 1539b edition (and reprints descended from it), these poems are inexplicably attributed to Jodocus Helmontanus, with no hint of the change.

[AFTER LUNCH WITH THE PONTIFEX, PASQUINO PRONOUNCED THE SQUIB APPENDED HERE.

Your bigwig-criticizing herald, your beloved poet,
      long liked by princes and the pontifex,
is suffering the Pelignian poet's punishment and disgrace:[24]
      he's suffering proscription, though it's a reward he deserves.
In so doing, he convinces dignitaries that dignitaries   5
      look puny when they demonstrate prompt and good approval.[25]]

THE END

      My kindly centurion[26] had the censor comb the pages,
and then entrusted it to the oversight of the printer.

JACOBUS DESCHAMPS'S POEMS TO THE READER

Our Porcius sang of pigs, while you sang of small things: *The Battle of Frogs and Mice.*[27]
      Thus does he recompense you, Homer, with a worthy reward.

ANOTHER

Homer sang of frogs, but Porcius sang of pigs
      after him. Clap and cheer for them both, please.

ANOTHER

Peruse the *Battles of the Pigs* while you're drinking, my drinker.[28]   5
      Our Porcius has planted goodies for a person drinking,
and the pigs' fights dispel all unhappiness:
      their poetry will make you want to read them aloud.
In just a few words, our poet recounted the pigs' glorious
      battles; when you finish reading, clap and cheer for our Porcius.   10

---

24 The "Pelignian poet" is Ovid, who was allegedly banished to the Black Sea by Augustus.
25 i.e., Placentius received no tip. If I interpret this correctly, *patres* (fathers) is the honorific title for leaders.
26 i.e., Placentius' religious superior in the Dominican order, who was responsible for obtaining the imprimatur.
27 *Croacus* was the Latin title that Elisius Calentius (1430–1503), the Italian humanist, gave Homer's *Batrakomyomachia*, published in 1448.
28 An allusion to the "Summons" on the title page.

THE AFTERMATH

On my return from Spain I thought of exposing the Soviet myth in a story that could be easily understood by almost anyone and which could be easily translated into other languages. ... I do not wish to comment on the work; if it does not speak for itself, it is a failure.

– George Orwell, preface to the Ukrainian translation of *Animal Farm* (see below)

What a mess! When our friend Placentius published *The Pig War* under a pseudonym, he had no inkling of the misunderstandings he'd let loose—the bristling, the squealing, the mudslinging, all of it far from home and among people he would never meet. *The Pig War* was meant for a local audience in Catholic Belgium, but within months it was bruising Protestant feelings on the far side of Germany, out amid the wine fields of Franconia. No one died, but within months at least one man's good name

> *sternitur infelix alieno vulnere*
> was laid low, unfulfilled, by a wound that was meant for another.[1]

And things got even crazier after that. Here's the untold story.

---

[1] Virgil *Aeneid* 10.781; tr. Ahl.

IN THE BEGINNING

Once upon a time in Belgium, there lived a Flemish Dominican priest named Johannes or Jan Leo Struyven (1500?-1538/9 or 1548). In those days it was customary for humanists to Latinize or Hellenize their last name, and since *Struif* was a Dutch word for a pastry, our author selected a Greek word for a cake, *plakous*, that had come into Latin as *placenta*. He thus christened himself *Placentius*.[2]

In time, though, people confused a placenta and a placebo. That is to say, in looking back, they assumed the friar's name had come from Latin *placere*, to please, and — Belgium being Belgium, half of which is French — they invented a ghost man by the name of Jean-Leo Plaisant. Since his presence still haunts card catalogues worldwide, let us dispel him once and for all. *Begone, Jean-Leo Plaisant! You never existed!*

Placentius spent a stint at the University of Leuven. He associated with an extinct residential college there known as "The Pig." In Latin it was called the *Paedagogium Porci* or *Porcianum Gymnasium*, and its residents called themselves *Porciani*. In Dutch, however, the college was known as *Het Varken*, and that name is, I suggest, our first solid clue that Placentius is unquestionably the author of *The Pig War*.[3]

I say that because the Dutch name alone can explain the mysterious letters HV in the author's cryptogram at the start of *The Pig War*, in which the initial letters spell out PLACENTIUSHV:

PRODITUR POETA

Plura Latent Animo Celata, Et Non Temeranda
Indiciis Ullis; Scilicet hoc volui.

THE POET UNMASKED

Many things lie hidden in my heart, and they mustn't be betrayed
by any hints; this was my choice, obviously.

And that identity is confirmed by the word *Porcianorum* — otherwise inexplicable — that introduces the second cryptogram at the front of *The Pig War*:

---

2   IJsewijn 1978; Bejczy 2009. Humanist names: Bernstein 2003.
3   *Porcianum gymnasium*: Van Iseghem and Speelman 1856, 16; *ex Porcianorum Gymnasio*: Hoffman, 1862.

> PRODITUR PATRONUS PORCIANORUM
> PRIMORDIALIBUS PUNCTIS
>
> Res Inamoena Caret Affectu, Laeta Decorem
> Omnimode Aspirat; Bellula Habe Ergo Rata.
>
> THE INITIALS UNMASK THE PORCIANI'S PATRON
>
> A gloomy thing lacks love, but a happy one radiates beauty
> in every direction, so choose pretty things.

This time the initials spell out RICALDOABHER, and they reveal that Placentius' "patron" at the *Paedagogium Porci* must have been (let me suggest) a man named Rikald (or Richard) van Heer. *Heer* is the name of a village outside Maastricht, and in a book of local history that Placentius had published in 1529, the year before *The Pig War*, I found a man with the same surname, though I could discover nothing else about him or his family. Whoever they were, neither man can have been much more than a local dignitary.[4]

Placentius' association with the *Paedagogium Porci* is one reason to suppose *The Pig War* started out as a satire of student life in Leuven, as Joseph IJsewijn suggested (but did not substantiate).[5] If so, the best hint in the text itself is the word *palaestra* in v. 24:

Praestat praelatis primam praebere palaestram.

For our bigwigs, it's preferable to offer a first-rate school.

But *palaestra* there might simply mean "level playing field," that is, meritocratic access to the privileges the hogs have been hogging. And as the story grows increasingly violent, it becomes harder and harder to key it closely to student-student or student-faculty relations.

At any rate, for the local Leuven readership Placentius originally intended, the identity of Rikald van Heer, and the "patronage" he offered him—presumably by hosting him—must have been obvious.

The Pig War did not remain a local production, though. Placentius had the text printed in Antwerp in 1530, just as he had had his local history printed there the year

---

4   Placentius 1529, Miii^r mentions a *Dominus a rivis, & ab Here, vir consiliis auxiliisque valentissimus* (the marginal note calls him a *Magnas ab Here*). At the back of the book, Placentius praises another individual by the same title.
5   IJsweijn 1976.

before.⁶ For two reasons, I suggest, this decision proved chaotic.

The first problem is that while going to print—as he himself says in the prologue—Placentius decided to add a page to the front of his book thanking his "patron." In lines 12-13, he declares *placuit parvam praefigere pugnae pagellam,* "I thought it would be nice to add this little page in to the front of the *War.*" And the fact that the prologue does appear on its own page in the original 1530 printings (though not in later reprints), proves that this is the correct interpretation of his words.

Placentius thanks this "patron" again in the *precatiuncula* at the back of the text, and, in the second edition of 1533, he mentions him yet again in the *Pasquinade.*

The problem is that the patron described in all these passages, however, is clearly not Rikald van Heer. As Ulysse Capitaine realized, he can only be Cardinal Erard von der Marck (1472-1538), the powerful prince-bishop of Liège whose long reign (1506-1538) was noted for peace, and who had "patronized" the publication of Placentius' 1529 catalogue of the bishops of Liège.⁷ Placentius' boner was in failing to make it clear that *The Pig War* now had two "patrons," and of different kinds: whereas van Heer was probably just a friend ("supporter") in Leuven, the powerful prince-bishop was someone Placentius hoped would pay for ("patronize") the cost of printing his poem.

Let me restate that point for emphasis: *the* patronus *identified in the cryptogram, Rikald van Heer, is not the* patronus *thanked in the prologue.* This is the point to grasp clearly and not lose sight of. Yet Placentius never says so.

When *The Pig War* got pirated and reprinted in Augsburg a few months later, this seemingly minor ambiguity was, I suggest, responsible for a great misunderstanding.⁸ Divorced of its context, German readers had no hope of understanding the (Dutch) abbreviation HV in the author's cryptogram. They also had no hope of understanding that the author had two patrons, not one, and can only have assumed that the powerful figure thanked for his "patronage" in the prologue and *precatiuncula* was a man whose name was Latinized as Ricaldus ab Her. And knowing nothing of the original context, they had no better hope of guessing what the target of the satire was. Despite all this, no one heeded the sage advice the Emperor Trajan once offered Pliny, that

> *sine auctore vero propositi libelli in nullo crimine locum habere debent.*
> anonymous books should play no part in accusations.⁹

---

6   Between September 1529 and 1534, Placentius moved from Leuven to Antwerp. We know this because the prefatory epistle in Placentius 1529 is signed *Louvanii decimo octavo Calendas Octobris, anno salutis 1529* (p. Avʳ), and by 1534, we find him teaching in Antwerp (Capitaine 1854-6, 6-8).
7   Capitaine 1854-6, 12. Erard's coat of arms appears on the title page of Placentius 1529.
8   It is clear that the 1530 Augsburg edition was pirated from the 1530 Antwerp edition and not the other way around; see the appendix.
9   Pliny *Epistle* 10.97.

Yet the libelous accusations happened immediately. As soon as the pirated Augsburg edition appeared in 1530, people began accusing Philip Melanchthon (1497-1560), the intellectual godfather of the Reformation and Martin Luther's right hand man, of writing *The Pig War*. Melanchthon denied it, though, and in turn credibly fingered a frenemy named Vincent Obsopoeus. He denounced the humanist in a pair of letters to Joachim Camerarius (1500-1574), who was then a rising star in European intellectual circles. In March of 1531, Melanchthon wrote:

> *Vidisti opinor carmen de porcis ab Obsopoeo porco, ut videtur, scriptum, in quo ego parum comiter pro nostra reconciliata gratia tractor.*

> I guess you've seen the pig poem, which that pig Obsopoeus apparently wrote. Seeing how the two of us had patched things up, I'm not treated very nicely in it.[10]

Two months later, in May, it was clear the controversy hadn't died down:

> *De carmine porcorum miror, quid his iudicii sit, qui me existimant auctorem esse, cum vel caeco apparere possit me praecipue ibi irrideri* καὶ κωμῳδεῖσθαι. *Obsopoeus est auctor, qui sui aucupis aucupatur gratiam.*

> I really wonder about the judgment of those who think *I* wrote the pig poem, when even a blind man can see I'm a special target of ridicule and mockery in it. Obsopoeus wrote it, and he's currying favor with his flatterer.[11]

Vincent Obsopoeus (?-1539) was a gifted translator, a superb Latin poet, a minor figure in the Reformation, and he was, by all accounts, an obnoxious guy. He delighted in twitting others for their failings, however minor.[12] It is only too believable that he could have written *The Pig War*. Five years earlier, he had angrily accused Melanchthon of passing him over while recommending people for jobs at the new Gymnasium in Nuremberg; Melanchthon had (said Obsopoeus) ridiculed him on various grounds, not least his drinking.[13]

---

10 MBW 1135, vol. 5, 84.
11 MBW 1152, vol. 5, 114. — I am not entirely sure what the last phrase means.
12 Fontaine 2020; Wilhelmi 2015.
13 Kobler 2014, 33 (1526).

Obsopoeus *did* like wine and joking about it, perhaps too much. In 1530, the same year *The Pig War* was published, he brought out a short *Rhapsodia in Ebrietatem*, and in 1536, he published a brilliant poem in three books titled *De Arte Bibendi, The Art of Drinking*.

Now, the *precatiuncula* that follows *The Pig War* contains several lines about the beneficial effects that wine exerts on poetry. The same idea is even more prominent in the *paraclesis pro potore* of the title page. This "Summons to the drinker" is a parody of the *paraclesis ad lectorem* ("Summons to the reader") in the preface to Erasmus' 1516 Greek edition of the New Testament:

> ### PARACLESIS PRO POTORE
>
> *Perlege porcorum pulcherrima proelia, potor.*
> *Potando, poteris placidam proferre poesim.*
>
> ### A SUMMONS TO THE DRINKER
>
> Peruse the pigs' glorious battles, my drinker!
> Drinking lets you produce placid poetry.

This cliché goes back to Horace (*Epistle* 1.19), but a clear parallel would soon appear in *De Arte Bibendi* (3.12):

> *post potum, melius carmina mille fluent.*
> After a drink [of wine], a thousand poems will flow better!

It is this casual attitude toward drinking, I suggest, that helped convince Melanchthon that Obsopoeus had written *The Pig War*, wrong though he was. That misunderstanding further poisoned their relationship and further embittered Obsopoeus, whose later life remained largely a series of frustrations and disappointments.[14]

It is also obvious why Melanchthon and his peers disregarded the attribution in the author's cryptogram of authorship to Placentius. First, they had never heard of this Flemish friar from Liège. Second, since the *H* and *V* were unintelligible, Melanchthon probably assumed *PLACENTIUS* itself was a mask for *VINCENTIUS*. And finally, anyone trying to determine the true identity of the patron (in reality, two patrons), was doomed to failure; the contradictory information about "the patron" implies the author

---

14   Fontaine 2020.

was secretly being funded by a wealthy and powerful aristocrat—and for who knows what nefarious purposes! It does not help that the cryptogram itself all but seems to say so:

> More things (*plura*) lie hidden in my heart, and they mustn't be betrayed
> by any hints; this was my choice, obviously.

In fact, it is easy to "find" an individual that fits the description of both patrons—that is, a man whose Latin name could be *Ricaldus ab Her* and who can be called (as the prologue calls him) *potentissimus*. I myself discovered an aristocratic family named von Merode that ruled parts of Belgium and Catholic western Germany at the time. In 1520 a scion named Rikald IV became *Reichsfreiherr* (overlord) and *Vogt* (patron) of Burtscheid, an old Roman town near Aachen whose Latin name is—get ready for it—Porcetum.[15] Anyone seeking to unmask this lord (*Herr*) of Porcetum as the patron of *The Pig War* might even find conclusive "proof" in the cryptogram's word *decorem*, which is nearly an anagram of *Merode*.

This is all hogwash, of course, and nothing but coincidence; the von Merode family has nothing to do with the poem. In the conspiratorial ferment of early Reformation Germany, though, it must have seemed intriguing, even reasonable. It must be what Melanchthon and his contemporaries thought. And it all goes to show, as the adage has it, that

> *Pro captu lectoris habent sua fata libelli.*
> A book's fate is determined by how readers interpret it.

LATER YEARS

Nearly every copy of *The Pig War* descends from early copies that were pirated and reprinted in Augsburg or Paris (see the stemma in the appendix). With nothing to go on, therefore, we see confusion about the author's identity already by the 17th century, when introductory notes to successive reprints profess total ignorance. Some claim the author had been one Petrus Porcius, alias Petrus Placentius or perhaps Placidus, a German, but no one knew for sure. These are just bad guesses based on no more than PLACENTIUS in the cryptogram and the original pseudonym, Publius Porcius.

It's no surprise, either, that in time even that pseudonym was misunderstood. The name "Publius Porcius" was originally supposed to evoke a name and writer of

---
15   Martin 1999, 169; Macco 1903, 139.

republican Roman times, like Marcus Porcius Cato. That is, it was supposed to be a *real* name, because in Roman times *Porcius* was no longer consciously associated with *porcus* (though it did ultimately derive from it).

As time passed, however, not only was the satirical point of the name lost, it turned back in on itself: a 1681 reprint of an anthology titled *Nugae Venales*, published in "Niverstadium" (i.e. "neverland," a made-up name), commissioned and included an illustration of the author *himself* as a hog (see figure 1).[16] It was frequently reprinted thereafter.

Figure 1. "Publius Porcius Poeta," from the 1681 edition of *Nugae Venales*

---

16   Abbreviated NV^2 in my stemma; see the appendix.

A CODA

Melanchthon and his contemporaries in Reformation Germany weren't the only ones to be driven mad by *The Pig War*. In 1975, Radu Constantinescu, a Romanian paleographer, concocted a harebrained theory:

> Probably enough, Jan van Leeuw (Johannes Leonis) of Sint Truiden was only the editor of a poem written by "P. Porcius poeta," i.e. Giannantonio de' Pandoni, a XVth c. Italian satirist, whose bawdy stanzas were never printed. ... [T]he satirist seems to describe the civil war in Rome under Eugenius IV; maybe, Van Leeuw alludes to some obscure events which occurred in Liège ca. 1521-1530.

That is, Constantinescu first misunderstood Johannes Leo Placentius' name as Johannes Leonis, and invented a ghost man he called "Jan van Leeuw."[17] He was then impressed that Giannantonio de' Pandoni (1409-1485) had also been known as Porcelio Pandone. Constantinescu then convinced himself that:

(1) de' Pandoni wrote *The Pig War*, that
(2) it allegorizes a civil war in Rome fought between 1434-1436, that
(3) Placentius silently discovered that poem in manuscript (where?) and "edited it," so that
(4) it *simultaneously also* allegorizes events in Belgium in Placentius' own time.

Naturally, of course, Constantinescu supplies a set of ingenious notes of his own devising to interpret everything for us.[18] Alas, this is tinfoil-hat territory. His hypothesis is absurd and false from start to finish.

The reality is that "privilege" and "oppression" will forever be infinite in their application. We would do well to remember, as many humanists have not, the wisdom of Sallust (*BC* 37.3):

> *Nam semper in civitate, quibus opes nullae sunt, bonis invident, malos extollunt, vetera odere, nova exoptant, odio suarum rerum mutari omnia student.*

> For in every state those who have no resources envy the productive citizens, praise the dregs, hate the traditional, pine for novelties and, due to dissatisfaction with their own lot, are eager for everything to be changed.[19]

---

17 Ijsweijn 1978.
18 Constantinescu 1975.
19 Tr. by Curtius 2017.

The envy of privileges, preferments, and perquisites is universal; we all feel it. So is the tendency to hog them; we all do. We always will. That is the story of *The Pig War*, and it brings us back to Orwell and the epigraph chosen for this essay.

Figure 2. *The Pig War*. From the 1681 edition of *Nugae Venales*; muskets do not appear in the poem.

In the late 19th century, English and French literary journals periodically rediscovered *The Pig War*, and copies are held in various English libraries. Although I cannot prove it, I consider it likely that Orwell knew or knew of it when he came to write *Animal Farm*, whose final sentence runs:

> The creatures outside looked from pig to man, and from man to pig, and from pig to man again; but already it was impossible to say which was which.

Animal Farm's stroke of genius lay in using pigs to allegorize human corruption, conflict, and revolutionary violence in a simple and transparent way. Anyone who compares it with *The Pig War* will discover numerous points of similarity. Both are satirical mini-epics, and their plots follow similar lines: the quick rebellion in *Animal Farm* chapter two; the pigs' consolidation of privileges in chapter three; the second battle of chapter four; the pigs' competitive speechmaking, in-fighting, violence, and increasing corruption in chapters five and six; and even chapter seven's framing of the pig Snowball as a dastardly traitor—all of these points are found in more or less identical form in *The Pig War*. Equally impressive are a number of details common to both: the pigs' use of written proclamations, the victory parade, even cannibalism.

Furthermore, in late 1946 Orwell wrote a friend a letter about *Animal Farm*. In it, he revealed,

> I meant the moral to be that revolutions only effect a radical improvement when the masses are alert and know how to chuck out their leaders as soon as the latter have done their job. The turning-point of the story was supposed to be when the pigs kept the milk and apples for themselves (Kronstadt).[20]

Although Orwell keys it to an anti-Soviet incident in 1921, what he calls the turning-point of the story has a parallel in *The Pig War* 165-171:

---

20 Davison 2013, 334.

> ### THE TWO-TIMING COLONELS STEAL THEIR SOLDIERS' PRIZES
>
> | | |
> |---|---:|
> | Next, stocks of prizes are procured for a great many pigs, but | 165 |
> | the leaders run up to the front and take most of the prizes. | |
> | They placate the powerless grunts with—alas!—promises: | |
> | two-timing them, they promise plunder better than | |
> | their own provisions. They offer the commoners | |
> | an I.O.U. to pay their pledges later, | 170 |
> | and the fight goes on. | |

That apart, given that *The Pig War* was written two and a half centuries before the French Revolution and in an era of perpetual monarchy, the text's emphasis on *the corruption of equality* among the pigs is, I suggest, far and away the most startling similarity. I submit that it influenced Orwell in the justly famous climax to his story (*Animal Farm* chapter 10):

> For once Benjamin [*the donkey*] consented to break his rule, and he read out to her what was written on the wall. There was nothing there now except a single Commandment. It ran:
>
> ALL ANIMALS ARE EQUAL
> BUT SOME ANIMALS ARE MORE EQUAL THAN OTHERS

To my mind, and perhaps to Orwell's, these words evoke the final agreement at the end of *The Pig War*:

> | | |
> |---|---:|
> | Accordingly, the commander and the spokesman proceed to make an agreement as the people look closely on: "Bigwigs shall divide and share in plunder with bigwigs on equal terms." For that reason, though, the young folks, | 240 |
> | joining together, cry out, "*Damn* these corrupt privileges!" | |

Finally, *The Pig War* contains another feature that may have caught Orwell's interest: namely, its Orwellian use of language. The vocabulary of *The Pig War* is necessarily limited; its genius lies in its constant use of the same words—e.g. *pro* or *porro* or *praescribere*—in different senses. Moreover, Latin famously contains a number of words that bear not just two different, but two *opposite* meanings: *sacer* (sacred/

accursed), *condere* (start/stop), *vacare* (relax/work hard), *profundere* (produce/throw away), and so on. *The Pig War* puts these contraries to spectacularly impressive use, and not least in *pinguis* (fat and lazy/bravehearted), the word Placentius daringly used of his powerful patron in the prologue. If Orwell did appreciate anything in this centuries-old poem, therefore, it was surely here—for in its language, I suggest, we discern the unmistakable roots of Newspeak.

Is it all a coincidence? In the Ukrainian preface to *Animal Farm*, Orwell tells readers he thought the story up in the late 1930s, long after his schooldays at Eton, "the most costly and snobbish of the English Public Schools":

> One day (I was then living in a small village) I saw a little boy, perhaps ten years old, driving a huge cart-horse along a narrow path, whipping it whenever it tried to turn. It struck me that if only such animals became aware of their strength we should have no power over them, and that men exploit animals in much the same way as the rich exploit the proletariat. I proceeded to analyse Marx's theory from the animals' point of view.

He explains that he did model the story on the Bolshevik Revolution, but only loosely:

> Although the various episodes are taken from the actual history of the Russian Revolution, they are dealt with schematically and their chronological order is changed; this was necessary for the symmetry of the story.

This vague account neither acknowledges nor precludes a connection with *The Pig War*. Since many scenarios seem possible, I hope Orwell scholars will study the parallels and decide.

FURTHER READING

Readers wanting a sense of Placentius' world are advised to start with *The Abyss* (*L'Œuvre au noir*), Marguerite Yourcenar's incomparable novel of life in 16th century Flanders. Those hankering for more puns might enjoy the *Canum cum catis certamen* of Henricus Harderus (1641-1683), a faint, fan-fiction imitation of *The Pig War*. It appears in the 1741 edition of *Nugae Venales* and many other reprints.

BIBLIOGRAPHY

Ahl, F. (tr.). 2007. *Virgil: The Aeneid*. Oxford: Oxford University Press.

Bejczy, I. P. 2009. "Johannes Placentius" in: Jan Bloemendal en Chris Heesakkers, eds., *Biobibliografie van Nederlandse Humanisten*. Digitale uitgave DWC/Huygens Instituut KNAW (Den Haag). (online at http://www.dwc.knaw.nl/placentius-johannes-1500-15389-of-1548/)

Bernstein, Eckhard. 2003. "Group Identity Formation in the German Renaissance Humanists: The Function of Latin," in: Eckhard Keßler and Heinrich C. Kuhn, eds., *Germania Latina. Latinitas teutonica*. Munich: Wilhelm Fink, vol. 1:375-386. (online at: http://www.phil-hum-ren.uni-muenchen.de/GermLat/Acta/Bernstein.htm)

Capitaine, U. 1854-6. "Notice sur Jean Placentius, poète et historien du XVIe siècle', *Bulletin de l'Institut archéologique liégeois* 2:299-314.

Constantinescu, Radu. 1975. "Manuscrise occidentale în bibliotecile românești. Bucuresti (sec. VIII-XVI)." *Revista Arhivelor* 52: 307-322.

Curtius, Quintus (tr.). 2017. *Sallust: The Conspiracy Of Catiline And The War Of Jugurtha*. CreateSpace Independent Publishing Platform.

Davison, Peter (ed). 2013. *George Orwell: A Life in Letters*. New York and London: Liveright.

Fontaine, Michael. 2020. *How to Drink: A Classical Guide to the Art of Imbibing*. Princeton University Press.

Hoffman, F. L. 1862. "Description de deux impressions de Thierry Martens." *Bulletin du Bibliophile Belge* 27:126-8.

IJsewijn. J. 1976. "Joannes Placentius, pugna porcorum per Placentium Poetam… Antwerpen…1533." In: *Tent. Cat. 550 jaar universiteit Leuven*, 207 (Leuven), 138-139.

IJsewijn. J. 1978. "The real name of Johannes Placentius." *Humanistica Lovaniensia* 25:283-4.

Kobler, B. 2014. *Die Entstehung des negativen Melanchthonbildes: Protestantische Melanchthonkritik bis 1560.* Tübingen: Mohr Siebeck.

Macco, H. F. 1903. "Schloss Kalkofen und seine Besitzer." *Zeitschrift des Aachener Geschichtsvereins* 25-6:133-64.

Marín Ibáñez, R. 1994. "Juan Luis Vives (¿1492?-1540)." *Perspectivas: Revista trimestral de educación comparada,* 3-4: 757-772.

Martin, G. 1999. *Histoire et généalogie de la maison de Merode.* Lyon: G. Martin.

MBW = Melanchthon, P., Scheible, H., & Thüringer, W. (eds.) 1977-. *Melanchthons Briefwechsel: krit. u. kommentierte Gesamtausg.* (1. Aufl.). Stuttgart-Bad Cannstatt: Frommann-Holzboog.

Nugae Venales: see the appendix.

Placentius, Joannes Leo. 1529. *Catalogus omnium antistitum Tungarorum Trajectensium ac Leodiorum et rerum domi bellique gestarum compendium.* Antwerp: Willem Vorsterman.

Van Iseghem, André F., and E. Speelman. 1856. *Biographie de Thierry Martens d'Alost, premier imprimeur de la Belgique.*

Wilhelmi, Thomas. 2015. "Opsopoeus, Vincentius" in: *Frühe Neuzeit in Deutschland 1520-1620. Literaturwissenschaftliches Verfasserlexikon,* vol. 4, Berlin, 664-673.

Yourcenar, Marguerite. 1976. *The Abyss.* New York: Farrar, Straus and Giroux.

For scholars

A NOTE ON THE LATIN TEXT

The text I present here is the first critical edition of the *Pugna Porcorum*. It is the first to appreciate that Placentius published two editions of the text, the first in Antwerp in 1530 and the revised second edition in Antwerp in 1533. In my text, I have freely regularized spelling, capitalization, and punctuation. I have added quotation marks and adopted small capital letters to indicate protests and proposals in indirect speech.

I have not bothered to include a critical apparatus because, with the few exceptions noted in footnotes to the text and repeated here, all variants are simply typos that corrupt the text. (They do indicate the relationships of dependence I have worked out below, but they are of no interest for construing the original text.)

THE MUTANTS

This list summarizes (1) my own conjectures or adoptions and (2) plausible differences between ANTWERP 1 (first edition) and ANTWERP 2 (the second edition). The few significant differences, which hint at revision rather than correction (27, 46, 231), are noted in footnotes to the translation. The rest look like simple corrections.

Line	Phontaine's text	ANTWERP 2	ANTWERP 1
Prologue 13	*Porcî* (genitive of *Porcius*) Phontaine	*porci*	*porci*
Main text 27	*potenti*	*potenti*	*patenti*
31	*perdere*	*perdere*	*pergere*
46	*percutientur*	*perpetientur*	*percutient(ur)*
79	*positos*	*porcos*	*positos*
134	*pergat* Phontaine	*perget*	*perget*
175	*protestabatur*	*protestabatur*	*pertrectabatur*
179	*poscent*	*poscent*	*pensent*
188	*poenis* deleted by Phontaine	*poenis*	*poenis*
212	*patente* (cf. 188, 219)	*patente*	*potente*
216	*pertraxerunt*	*pertraxerunt*	*protraxerunt*
231	*perdendo*	*praefecto*	*perdendo*
240	*pubes*	*pubes*	*plebes*
Liminary poem 6	*potanti* (conjecture by Cap)	N/A	*pedentis*

THE GREAT SOW AND HER FIVE LITTERS

The following chart delineates the five litters as I have reconstructed them. I believe all editions of the *Pugna* can be slotted into the following stemma. The lines of descent reconstructed here rest on a small number of typos variously shared or silently corrected among the editions. I have assembled a list, but since nearly all are obvious (they result in non-words or ungrammatical variants), they are not worth listing here. Instead, I have determined that the minimal dispositive traits listed below will permit owners unsure of any reprint to determine its line of descent.

Litter	Birthmarks
ANTWERP 1	*Placentium* in the last verse of the *Precatiuncula*, and/or *personavit* (not *personuit*) *Placentius post pocula;* contains the liminary poems and attributes them to Jacobus Deschamps
ANTWERP 2	The long title *Pugna Porcorum per Placentium* (instead of *Porcium*) *Poetam postremo Pasquillus post prandium pontificis prelegens Poema*, contains these supplementary materials, and has *Placentium* in the last verse of the *Precatiuncula*.
AUGSBURG	*Placentum* in the last verse of the *Precatiuncula*.
BASEL	Contains new prefatory material by Gilbertus Cognatus
PARIS 2	Contains the liminary poems and attributes them to Jodocus Helmontanus

PIGNORA PUGNAE PORCORUM PROLATA PIGENDA: DETAILS OF *THE PIG WAR'S* MISBEGOTTEN OFFSPRING

I have autopsied the underlined editions and infer the contents of the rest from published reports (viz. Cap or library card catalogues). Since Ant^1 is the Great Sow (archetype) and Ant^2 is Placentius' revised second edition, only editions in the ANTWERP 2 litter are of scholarly interest today (NB most reprints not listed here belong to the PARIS 2 litter—the runts.)

name	Date and publisher	litter
1550	1550, no indication	AUGSBURG
Anon	after 1553, probably 1623; a copy written by hand on the fly-leaves of a printed copy of Nicholas Borbonius' *Nugae* (Basel 1553) (cf. Constantinescu 1975, 316)	AUGSBURG
Ant[1]	August 1530, Antwerp, Simon Cock	ANTWERP 1
Ant[2]	March 1533, Antwerp, Simon Cock	ANTWERP 2
Aug[1]	1530 Augsburg 1, Steiner? [floral cover & typo in the imprimatur]	AUGSBURG
Aug[2]	1530 Augsburg 2, Steiner? [people & animals on cover; no imprimatur]	AUGSBURG
Bas[1]	1546 Basel, Jacob Parcus	BASEL
Bas[2]	1547 Basel, Jacob Parcus	BASEL
Bas[3]	1552 Basel (in *Acrostichia*), Jacob Parcus	BASEL
Bru	1831 Brunswick, Gravenhorst/Typis orphanotrophii	PARIS 2
Cap	1856 "edition" of Capitaine	PARIS 2
Col	1566 Cologne	ANTWERP 2
Han	1619 Hanover (in Caspar Dornavius (ed.), *Amphitheatrum sapientiae Socraticae joco-seriae*), typis Wechelianis	AUGSBURG
Lon[1]	1586 London	ANTWERP 2
Lon[2]	1831 London (in *Specimens of Macaronic Poetry*), Richard Beckley	PARIS 2
Lov	1546 Leuven, J. Wellaeus	BASEL
Neo	1540 Nijmegen, Petrus Elfenius.	ANTWERP 2
NV[1]	1642, no indication of place (in *Nugae Venales*)	PARIS 2
NV[2]	1681 "Niverstadium" (in *Nugae Venales*); first to include the two illustrations	PARIS 2
Par[1]	1539 Paris 1, H. Gormontius	ANTWERP 1
Par[2]	1539 Paris 2, A. Bonnemere	PARIS 2
Sch	1786 Schleusingen	PARIS 2

PROLIFERATION OF THE PIGS

NB: Some siblings in this stemma probably descend from a sibling rather than their parent, and, though it little matters, various editions in the **AUGSBURG** litter might come from **Aug¹** rather than **Aug²**.

It is important to notice that hardly any copies descend from **Ant²**, Placentius' revised second edition: just those underlined. To put it differently, almost all extant copies of the *Pugna Porcorum* descend from increasingly corrupt printings of the **Great Sow**, nearly half of them from the pirated Augsburg editions.

Meanwhile, any copy that contains the two illustrations of the author and the pig battle (reprinted here in the afterword) descends from NV^2 or one of its reprints (in 1703, 1720, 1741), rather than an earlier reprint of NV^1 (1644, 1648).

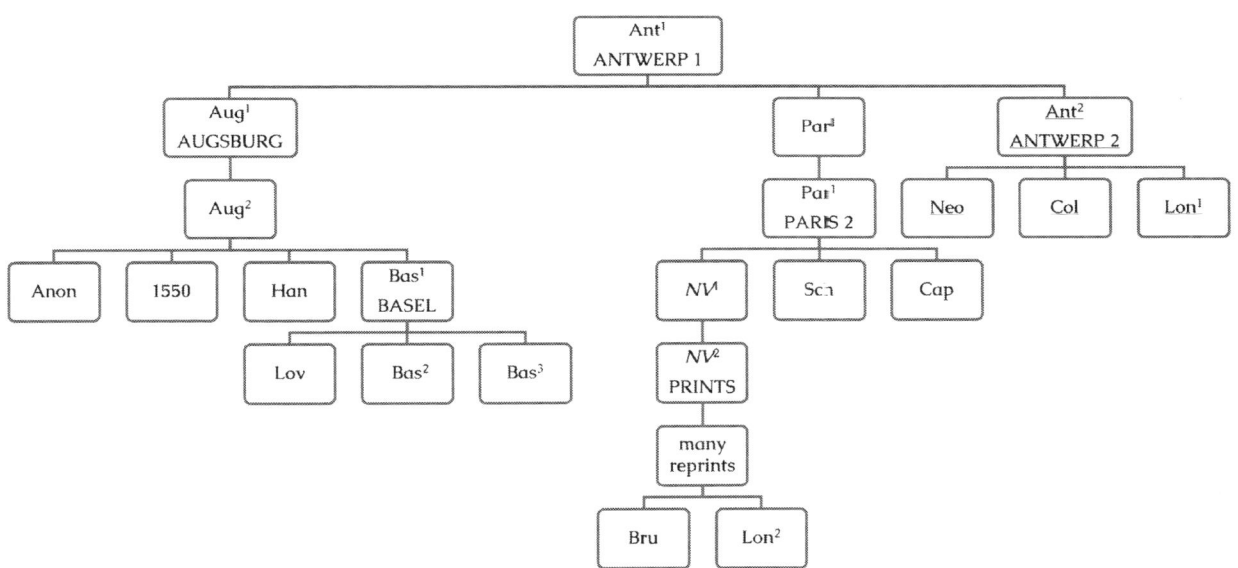

PRAISES 'PON *PIG WAR* PUBLISHED

"Among the delights of humanistic scholarship is stumbling upon an obscure literary treasure. Michael Fontaine pleasingly shows us a work that is ingeniously constructed, eternally insightful about the human condition, and—perhaps—an influence on one of the most famous novels of the 20th century. This is an unusual, enjoyable, and edifying effort."

– Steven Pinker, Johnstone Professor, Harvard University, and the author of *The Language Instinct* and *Enlightenment Now*.

"In this pioneering and pathbreaking edition of this pre-modern poem, pugnacious porcine epic cum political parable, Fontaine is playful rather than pedantic or plodding in his prose paraphrase and prodigious scholarship, producing pleasing and plucky prose out of a problematic Pig(gish)-Latin prickly to parse. He even proposes the poem as a possible prototype for Orwell's popular *Animal Farm*. Plaudits to this praiseworthy project."

– A.E. Stallings, author of *Like*.

"Passionate, persuasive, politically provocative, *The Pig War* is a gem of a text. The conflict between selfish fat hogs and impatient piglets on the up is an evergreen topic, but the experimental form, a daring tautogram, places this little poem in a category of its own with Queuneau and Eco. Michael Fontaine has done a fantastic service to lovers of all forms of Latin—ancient and modern—by rescuing from oblivion this brilliant instance of political satire and poetic inventiveness, establishing a critical text, and providing a crisp English translation—the first ever. *Perlecta plaudite pugna!*"

– Alessandro Schiesaro, Professor of Classics, Manchester University

"In putting pen to paper, Michael Fontaine shows off his extraordinary chops as an artful interpreter of language and history alike. And in today's age of plutocrats, populism and Orwellian dangers, his translation and analysis of *The Pig War* couldn't be more timely. It's also a lot of fun."

– John Pollack, author of *The Pun Also Rises*

"What a fascinating tale of an curious poem. Professor Fontaine discusses it with evident joy. Anyone interested in the quirks of literature will enjoy this."

– Thomas E. Ricks, author of *Churchill and Orwell*

The Piglets and the "P":

Undaunted by an ancestor's alliterative Latinity,
Now Mike's interpretation takes it almost to infinity.
The thrill of the impossible made actual in every line
Will give you an experience of poetry that's porcelline.

Come, connoisseurs of curious, proponents of all paradox,
For form effacing function, scan these swinish soldiers' simple socks!
Evincing education, even laced with incredulity,
a dull dubiety of dons is leavened with garrulity.

– Nicholas Ostler, author of *Ad Infinitum: A Biography of Latin* and *Empires of the Word: A Language History of the World.*

Pugna Placentî Porcorum (Phaedro placuisset) phabula, proloquitur: pende problema potens.

Phontanus Parthicé